TAKE 2

Eleven Contemporary or Traditional Two-Color Quilts

by JOANNA BROOKS MYRICK

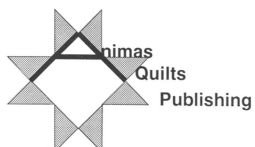
Animas Quilts Publishing

600 Main Ave.
Durango, CO. 81301
(303) 247-2582

TAKE 2

Copyright © 1994
by Joanna Myrick

Animas Quilts Publishing
600 Main Ave.
Durango, CO 81301
(303) 247-2582

ISBN: 1-885156-09-X

Printed on Recycled Paper

Cover Quilt:
  Georgia On My Mind
    Joanna Myrick
Back Cover:
  Stark Reality
    Joanna Myrick
Center Cover:
  Starry Nights and Irises
    Pieced by Linda Soenen
    Quilted by Janice Minyard

CREDITS:

Editor	Kim Gjere
Asst. Editor	Barbara Morgan
Graphics	Jackie Robinson
Photographer	Christopher Marona

ABOUT THE AUTHOR

Joanna Brooks Myrick has been quilting since 1982 and teaching since 1988. In 1991 she opened a shop, North County Quiltworks, in Atascadero, California where she continues to teach and share her love of quilting. She likes to say that her Aunt Polly gave her wings, but Mary Ellen taught her to fly! Joanna feels that she really became a "quilter" after attending a lecture by ME in early 1984. Many of the techniques in this book were learned at "It's Okay" seminars and Joanna thanks Mary Ellen Hopkins for her unique and humorous contribution to quilting.

Born in Atchison, Kansas and raised in Southern California, Joanna and her husband, Larry, moved to the Central Coast of California in 1978. She has two handsome sons, David and Donn, a beautiful daughter, Becky, and an angelic daughter-in-law, Kim. She is known as Granny "J" to Amanda and Nicholas, the two cutest grandchildren in the whole world.

ACKNOWLEDGMENTS

I would like to offer my thanks to everyone who encouraged me as this book was conceived and became reality. To all the piecers and quilters, a resounding thank you. To Teri Gentry, for doing the "B" word (basting) with a smile and to Paula Fuller, for sewing all those circles, you both are great.

My warmest thanks and deepest gratitude to Janice Minyard, for making quilts, machine quilting, figuring yardages, helping me with the mathematics side of all my quilting projects and binding. But most of all for just being there and gently prodding me along with her kind words of encouragement. (It never hurts to have a math teacher for a best friend.)

A special hug for Larry, aka "Dear", for helping me to make my wishes come true!

I love you all.

DEDICATION

This book is dedicated to some "mighty fine women." My mother, Gladys Ward Brooks, who so lacked in sewing skills that we celebrated when she replaced a button. My aunt, Pauline Hale Hayes, who was so accomplished in the womanly arts that my mother didn't need to be. My mother-in-law, Kathryn Koch Myrick, whose "financial aid" made North County Quiltworks a reality.

INTRODUCTION

The inspiration for this book came from my efforts to use an all-over floral print containing nearly every color imaginable. Nothing would complement this fabric but black, a deep, dark black. Of course, my first thought was to go through my quilting books in search of a pattern. I was sure that there would be several two fabric quilts to feed my desire. I was wrong.

For the last several years quilters have been using many fabrics in their quilt tops. Sometimes it seems as though there is a contest to see how many different fabrics one can use without making a scrap or charm quilt! As I designed "Georgia On My Mind" I realized how fresh and restful the two fabric quilt appeared. Now, for the rest of the story.

Taking the vividly colored fabric as my accent fabric and a deep, dark black as my background fabric I was drawn to the poppy design in the fabric. It reminded me of a Georgia O'Keefe painting thus the name "Georgia On My Mind." However, using the poppy required the dreaded "A" word - applique!

I "build" my quilts on a design wall. After appliqueing the poppy I put it on the wall and stared at it for several days and weeks. It seemed like months. My friends and customers were continuously asking what I was going to do and I had no idea! This design business is not for the weak at heart. It was really hard work designing "Georgia", but also very rewarding.

Finally I decided to use my favorite pattern, Ohio Star. All the stars would be different because of the variety of color in the fabric. I envisioned a medallion surrounded by Ohio Stars. It didn't work - the stars and the poppy seemed to have no connection. I tried changing the position of the medallion. On point, straight, off center, centered - what a pain! At that point I decided Ohio Star wasn't enough to build this particular quilt around. So, I started making pinwheels and arranging them around the medallion. I planned to make them in ascending size from the center out. Didn't work. By this time I was ready to toss the whole project in the corner (that's where all my piecing problems go and believe me, the pile gets pretty high!). But that poppy kept calling to me.

Six months had gone by and all I had were eight Ohio Star blocks and a zillion pinwheels. Everyday someone asked how I was coming on my "big red flower" quilt. Grrrrr.

In a design dervish, I decided to put everything on the wall. I put up the poppy medallion, the Ohio Stars and the pinwheels. Someone commented that they liked the look of the pinwheels at the bottom and someone else said it looked bottom heavy. Another voice piped up and said "Yes, but the stars at the top balance it." Finally, it came to me. Pinwheels at the bottom, which would not be square, the poppy in the center on point, and Ohio Stars with a few pinwheels at the top. It gave a sense of churning motion at the bottom, flowering into life, and a lightness at the top. I was so moved I wrote a poem...

We begin as an array of
   elements,
flower into life and return to the
  elements as stars...

We are all colors
and yet the same...

The earth is our home
as is the sky.

The spinning pinwheels below
and the floating stars above
signify our ties to the earth
and our eventual ascent to the
  heavens

    ...life is a never
       ending circle.

How profound! I wax poetic whenever the mood strikes me and every once in a while I hit a home run. "Georgia On My Mind" is my home run.

FABRIC...THE QUILTERS MEDIUM OF EXPRESSION

Which came first: fabric or color? To a quilter the question is moot. Color and fabric are one and the same. Fabric to quilters is like paint to an artist, wood to a carpenter, stone to a sculptor. It is that with which we express and create our artistic impressions.

Because we are all individuals, color is an intensely personal subject. We use color everyday. We get dressed. We decorate our homes. Admittedly, some of us do it a little snazzier than the rest, but we do it! Choosing fabric for a quilt is so personal that I can't imagine asking someone to select fabric for me. However, I have learned that we all discover that "color coordinator" inside ourselves with practice and a little success. It just takes one quilt, greeted with oohs and aahs, to convince us that yes, we can do this! We are color experts.

My advice to beginners is to find one fabric that you love. I have built this lesson into my beginning classes and also use it as a lecture. It's called "Find the One You Love." We all can walk into a fabric store and choose one fabric that we just love and usually it will contain several colors to coordinate with.

Have you ever looked at a quilt and wondered why a particular fabric was used? I'm sure the quilter spent a great deal of time matching a small part of the print. However, from a distance of three feet or more it is impossible to see what it matches and it distracts from the overall effect. It is very tempting to matchy-match a color, but please, refrain. Look at the primary fabric from a distance of at least three feet. If you can't see a color clearly, don't try to match it.

Many of us have a strong dislike of certain colors. Who knows why? Maybe your archenemy in high school wore a certain shade of pink, perhaps your mother painted your room a screaming yellow and your taste for those colors is forever tainted. Who cares? Just be aware that as a quilter, fabric and color are your mediums of expression and you must open your mind, and yes, your heart to those "yucky" colors. Here are some things to keep in mind when selecting fabric for your quilts:

- Clash is not a four letter word. It is much more effective to be just a shade off the color you are trying to match. This slight variation in color adds a sparkle and keeps things from mushing together.

- You can mix plaids, geometrics, prints, stripes, large florals and checks, no matter what your mother told you!

- You need some "uglies" to make the pretty look pretty. If every fabric in your quilt is gorgeous, it's like having too much candy. You need some "roughage" in your fabric diet. Pea green, mustard yellow, orange, shocking pink, vivid violet and drab gray each have a place in the quilters palette.

- You are not decorating the house every time you make a quilt. You wouldn't buy a painting because it matches your sofa would you? (Please, say no!)

- Sometimes a color you thought you didn't like calls to you, so use it and consider it a growing experience in your journey as a quilter.

- There are some basic "go with everything" colors. They are navy, red, turquoise, forest green, eggplant, and taupe.

- Backgrounds do not have to be muslin, solids or anything that reads as a solid. Some great quilts have used huge florals, geometrics, and plaids as backgrounds. Be daring!

Beginning quilters are sometimes amazed, if not shocked, to see how much fabric I have amassed in my ten plus years of quilting. They also find it hard to believe that I buy fabric without a specific project in mind. My stash inspires me and comforts me. I know that I can always build a quilt right out of my stash. My problem is I'm afraid if I use it, it will be gone, so I'm reluctant to use some fabrics knowing I will never find them again. I have learned to buy lots of anything that I truly love and that there are always going to be new fabrics out there to choose from.

Purchasing fabric is a big investment, gone are the days of $1.99 a yard cottons. On the plus side, we now have better quality cotton fabric, with brighter, truer, and faster colors in a vast array of patterns. Although I began buying quarter yards, I soon found that a quarter, even a fat quarter, was not enough to make a quilt. Often fabrics are not reprinted and it is very frustrating to find that you need more two years after the original purchase. My advice is to buy a little long. My own personal purchasing philosophy (don't tell Dear this) is to buy at least a yard of everything. If I really like it a lot I buy 2-3 yards and if I love it I buy at least 3-5 yards, whichever the budget allows. When I see a fabric that would make a great background, border, or back I buy at least four yards. Often, bolts on the sale table will make great backings for quilts and you can buy in quantity because the price is lower.

A WORD ABOUT VALUE

While color is important to successful quilt-making, value is really what it is all about. Without value in our fabric selection, our pieced pattern fails to emerge.

Value is the lightness or darkness of a color or hue. A hue or color has numerous values ranging from the palest of lights to the darkest of darks. Value is a relative term, because a color can be light, medium, or dark depending upon its relationship and nearness to another color.

A shade is a darker value of a hue, having had black added to it. Shades are low in value. Navy blue is a shade of blue; burgundy is a shade of red.

A tint is a lighter value of a hue having had white added to it. Tints are high in value. Lavender is a tint of violet and peach is a tint of orange.

Value defines shapes within a pattern and provides contrast. Light values advance and dark values recede. Color values can indicate depth for dimensional effects in patterns. Rearrangement of value can provide variations and possibilities for more interesting composition.

To determine value, look at the fabrics as if they are in black and white. This can be done by squinting or using a value filter. It can also be done with a photocopy. Fabrics that photocopy the same have the same value.

Make a mock-up of your block using fabric and a glue stick. Photocopy the block in black and white. This will show you the value differences or lack of them in your fabric choices. If poor value change is evident you can then substitute before making the quilt.

Sometimes a quilter wishes to have very little contrast or value change in a quilt. Many Amish quilts are low in value and contrast. Watercolor type quilts depend on the similarity in value for transitions. This can be very effective. It also allows us to substitute another print of the same value when we run short. The substitution is hardly noticeable if the values of both fabrics are the same. The quilts in Take 2 require fairly high contrast since only two fabrics are used.

There...now you know about fabric and Take 2 has made it a piece of cake because after finding the "one you love" you only have to find one other. Remember that it needn't be a solid and a loud, busy print. Only two of the quilts in this book use a solid. The "one you love" may be either the background or the accent, depending on the fabrics and the design chosen.

Beginners will find this a way to make stunning quilts that really let the fabric do the work. More experienced quilters have found it to be a challenge to only use two fabrics. So, I invite you, Take 2 and build a great quilt!

Piecing requires little more than the ability to cut and sew a straight line. All the quilts in this book were built using template-free methods. Good tools will help you to do this more accurately and much faster. Buy the best tools you can afford. It saves money in the long run since you won't have to replace inferior products that don't work well or that don't hold up to constant use.

The necessary tools for Take 2 quilts are: sewing machine (in good working order), rotary cutter, self-healing mat, acrylic ruler, a steam iron, a design wall, and a good lamp.

You don't need a special sewing machine for piecing and quilting, any machine with forward and reverse will do. However, be sure to treat your sewing machine like the tool that it is. Oil it frequently, dust it often and change the needle! Yes, change the needle, even if it's not broken. I change mine about every 8-12 hours of sewing time or whenever I begin a new, large project. You will be amazed at what a difference a new needle can make.

Rotary tools are expensive, but well worth the cost. They allow you to cut more fabric, faster and with more accuracy. I recommend the large cutter, the 18" x 24" mat, and a good ruler. The ruler should have 1/8" marks and angles of 45° and 60°. Later, you will want to add other rulers as you need them for special projects. Square rulers are nice to have, especially the 6-1/2" and 12" sizes.

Pressing is a very important aspect of successful piecing. It requires a good steam iron and a sturdy surface to press on. Pressing is not ironing! Pressing does not distort the fabric, ironing can and will. Press from the top of your piece and press to the dark side, whenever possible. Sometimes you have to press the way it wants to go regardless of color. I press after every seam and often find that when there is a problem with fit, there is a fold or a crease at the seam line. This can affect the size of the pieces. Also be aware of and careful of bias edges on triangles, diamonds, pyramids, etc. Aggressive ironing can and will stretch them and nothing will repair the damage. Just cut new ones (another reason to buy extra yardage).

A design wall is a valuable tool for a quilter. I "build" my quilts on the wall before I sew anything together. It is simply a piece of fleece pinned to the wall. The fleece holds the pieces of the blocks without pinning, making it easy to change things around during the design process. If you don't want a fleece covered wall make a portable design wall by covering a piece of corefoam with fleece. Slip it under the bed when you aren't using it.

Good, bright light is a must for piecing and quilting. I like to use an adjustable lamp on my sewing table and a floor lamp beside my chair for quilting. The lights on sewing machines are not adequate for accuracy. Lamps are available in all price ranges. Check those ads!

Finally, you will need basic sewing supplies: thread, pins, needles, reverse sewer (seam ripper), thimble, pencils, graph paper, colored pencils and a notebook or file folder to hold your ideas and quilt plans.

CONSTRUCTION ZONE
Caution! Quilter at Work

Sample Block

I always begin with a sample block. This is even more important when making Take 2 quilts. If the two fabrics aren't going to work together it's better to find out right away, before cutting into all the fabric. There are several other reasons to make a sample block. They are:

- To check for value and color placement.
- To find and eliminate construction booby traps.
- To estimate yardage requirements.
- To simply see if you like it
  (do the fabrics chosen work well together).

Those of us who are mathematically challenged should always make a sample block. We have a way of vastly under-estimating or over-estimating our yardage. I prefer to know in advance, and in the privacy of my own home, when I've pulled a real boner, mathematically speaking. Also, fabrics that look great together on the bolt often don't work well together when cut up. Sample blocks that don't become quilt blocks make wonderful pillows, pot-holders, and mini wall hangings. Non-quilters are especially pleased to receive these "boo-boos" for gifts. They don't know any better and are very easily impressed. Sample blocks...the secret to my success!

While piecing the sample block you can determine which parts can be speed pieced. Speed piecing means chaining all like pieces through at one time. This is a great time saver and very useful when making an entire quilt of the same block.

Every quilter has their own way of working. I like to cut a little, piece a little, cut a little, piece a little, etc. My best friend, Janice, cuts everything at once and then speed pieces, pedal to the floor until she's done. Whatever works for you, do it!

Seam allowance causes a lot of discussion among quilters. Usually, if all the piecing will be done on the same machine and all the blocks are the same, you can use the side of the presser foot as a guide. Technically, a 1/4" seam allowance is desired, but it may be easier and more accurate to use the presser foot as a guide. The seam allowance can also be marked with tape, moleskin, etc.

I took Home Economics for several years and I hated pinning! I don't know why; it probably slowed me down. For a long time I did not do any piecing that required accuracy to the point of pinning. Eventually I wanted to do Radiant Stars and other more challenging projects. I began pinning and, Voila!, my piecing improved tremendously.

Quilter Drawing: Christina Eisenberg

ROTARY CUTTING

Rotary cutting is to quilters what sliced bread is to sandwich making. It does the job faster and more accurately. Here is how it's done:

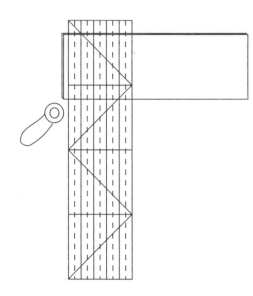

- Fold fabric selvage to selvage. Don't worry about having it straight on either end.

- Fold once again away from you, placing the first fold over the selvage.

- Smooth fabric after each fold to find and smooth out wrinkles. Wrinkles cause distortion in the cut of the strip. If the strip has a bulge then the fold has a wrinkle.

- Place fold of fabric on grid line of mat. This is one straight edge. Place ruler over the fabric and cut the uneven edges off. This is the second straight edge.

- Right handed quilters will have the fabric to the right of the ruler and those who are left handed will have the fabric to the left.

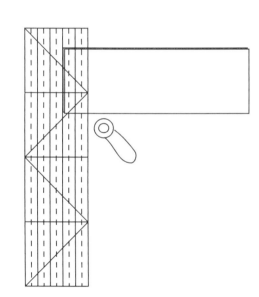

- Use the ruler's measurements to find the size of cut required and cut the strip. Remember the fabric strip being cut is under the ruler when the cut is made.

- It is necessary to check the straight edge on the cut side occasionally, and recut if necessary.

- Always cut away from you, running the blade of the cutter along the side of the ruler. Hold the ruler firmly in place. Never leave the rotary cutter open when laying it down; it is very sharp.

WHICH TRIANGLE IS WHICH?

The most important lesson I've learned about piecing is where to use which triangle. Piecing consists mainly of half-square and quarter-square triangles, squares, and rectangles. Using the correct triangle in the block is very important.

Half-square triangles are used when the short side of the triangle will be on the outside edge of the square. An example would be the Pinwheel block which is constructed entirely of half-square triangle units.

These are quick to cut from strips. Add 7/8" to the finished size of the square needed and cut the strip this width. Next cross-cut the strips into squares. To make the half-square units layer a light square upon a dark square, right sides together, and draw a diagonal line connecting opposite corners. Sew 1/4" on both sides of the line and cut on the line.

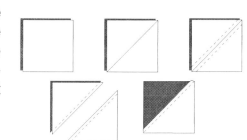

Press to the dark side and, Presto!, you have half-square triangle units.

If a large number of units using the same fabrics are needed, layer the lighter fabric on the darker, right sides together and draw a grid the size of the finished square plus 7/8". Draw diagonal lines across all squares on the grid as shown at right, and sew 1/4" on both sides of the drawn diagonal line. Cut on all diagonal lines.

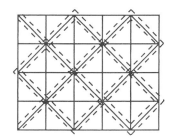

There is also commercial triangle paper available which already has the grid drawn on it. There are a variety of sizes. With this paper all you need to do is layer the two fabrics, pin the paper onto the fabrics, sew on the sewing lines, cut on the cutting lines, then easily remove the paper.

Quarter-square triangles are used when the long side of the triangle will be on the outside of the block, as in the Ohio Star in Georgia on My Mind on page 53.

Add 1-1/4" to the finished size of the squares and cut a strip that size. Cross-cut into squares. Layer the lighter fabric on the darker fabric, right sides together, and draw a diagonal line from corner to opposite corner. Sew 1/4" on both sides of the line and cut on the drawn line. Press open.

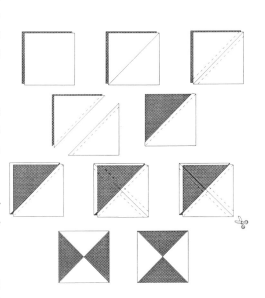

Layer two of these units together, seams together, with opposite colors facing. Draw a diagonal line on the top layer from corner to opposite corner, perpendicular to the seam line. Stitch 1/4" on both sides of the drawn line, then cut on the line. Press open.

When making many of these units consider drawing a grid or using the commercial quarter-square triangle paper as explained for the half-square triangles above.

It is very important to use the correct triangle for the block you are making. If you don't, the bias edge of the triangle will be on the outside edge of the block and will streeeeetch. Uh, oh! Time to unsew.

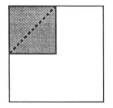

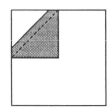

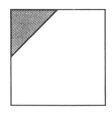

FOLDED CORNER TRIANGLE UNITS

These units make starrier stars because the points won't get cut off, resulting in stubby stars. They are a snap to make and eliminate dealing with teeny tiny triangles. Mary Ellen Hopkins developed this method, calling the folded corners "connectors." This method was used to make "Chapman College", page 16; "Hidden Stars", page 24; and Robert's Bright Idea, page 35. Try it!

- Place a small square, right sides together against the background piece, in the corner where the "triangle" is wanted.

- Stitch diagonally across the small square from corner to corner as shown to the left.

- Trim away excess (back) of corner square if desired. However, do not trim or cut the background fabric. This is used for sizing the blocks and must remain true.

- Press the corner open.

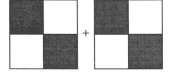

TWOSIE - FOURSIE CONSTRUCTION METHOD

Mary Ellen also taught me this at an "It's Okay" seminar. This method eliminates the chance of sewing the wrong blocks together. It also makes matching corners and seams much easier. First sew all the blocks together in pairs (twosies). Then sew the pairs together (foursies). Continue on to sets of eight, sixteen, etc. Two, Four, Six, Eight...who do we appreciate? ME, of course.

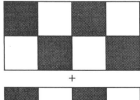

THE THREE B'S OF QUILTING......
BORDERS, BACKS & BINDINGS

BORDERS

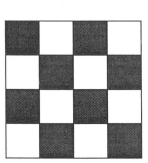

Once the blocks have been sewn together it's time to decide on the borders. Some quilts are fine without borders while others need one or more. Audition them like the mats of finely framed artwork until you find the number and width of the borders the quilt requires. Borders may also be pieced as in "Chapman College", page 16, where Flying Geese blocks were used to make the border. The "Irish Chain", page 13, also has multiple borders including a pieced one. Sometimes just a different corner block in the border, as in "Hidden Stars", page 24, is enough to add interest without piecing the entire border. Be creative but remember, every quilt does not need a border.

Measure border strips
through the center
of the quilt

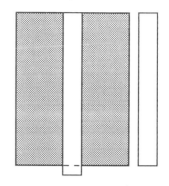

Oh, say...do they wave? The borders I mean. This happens when the edges of the quilt have been measured to determine border length. Instead measure through the center. This is the true measurement and sometimes the quilt has to be eased in to fit the border or the border eased in to fit the quilt. If wavy borders are a problem, remember to always measure through the center of the quilt.

BACKING

Often, we are tempted to use muslin, solids and other plain fabrics on the backs of our quilts. But I say, let the back be as interesting as the front! It adds some excitement to use a completely different fabric when the quilt is thrown back on a bed or over the arm of the sofa. For the beginning quilter it's also nice to use a busy print on the back so the quilting stitches can't be so easily scrutinized.

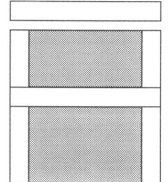

Backs may also be pieced. It's a great way to use leftover blocks from the front or use some large pieces of your stash. Very creative, it's called back art. I call it the flip side.

BINDING

The binding will be added after the quilt is quilted. It is the part of a quilt that gets the most wear. So, it is very important that you not pull the back to the front for binding. It will wear and erode into the back of your quilt. A binding can be replaced but it is impossible to replace the back of a quilted quilt.

I don't use bias bindings unless I am binding a quilt with a curved edge. Straight grain bindings have always worked for me and they use less fabric. Measure the perimeter of the quilt and add 9". Cut enough 2-1/2" strips, estimating 40" per strip and sew them together diagonally. Press seam open to eliminate bulk. This diagonal seam is less noticeable than a straight seam would be.

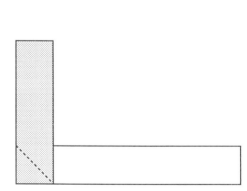

Press this long strip lengthwise, wrong sides together, and sew to the quilt using your favorite binding technique.

TO HAND QUILT
OR NOT TO HAND QUILT

I love to hand quilt and I like to leave large empty spaces to quilt in. "Hidden Stars" (wall hanging size), "Chapman College" and "Stark Reality" were made with large corners to hand quilt in. However, most of the quilts in this book were intended to be machine quilted due to the construction methods. Machine quilting can be done "in the ditch" (seamline) or free hand. Practice is the key to the latter.

Before quilting, whether by machine or hand, the top must be marked and the layers basted together. Using a stencil or a ruler, mark the design on the top with a pencil, chalk marker or any water soluble marker intended for this use.

Hand quilting requires thread basting. Place the backing fabric, which is at least 4" larger all around the quilt, wrong side up on a table. Using masking tape, tape the backing fabric to the table. It should be very smooth. Lay the batting on top of the backing and smooth out any wrinkles. (Sometimes a batt needs to lay out over night to unwrinkle.) Center the quilt on the batting and backing. Pin from the center out with long straight pins, smoothing with your hands to remove wrinkles. Using a long needle, (I use a milliners needle) begin at the center and baste with long stitches diagonally from center to each corner. Then baste down the center and across the center. Finally, baste in a 2" grid both vertically and horizontally. It seems like a lot but it really makes a difference in the finished quilt.

Begin hand quilting in the center of the quilt. I like to have a practice piece to quilt on for ten minutes or so until I get warmed up. Place the quilt in a hoop or frame and check for wrinkles on the back. Have the piece firm but not tight. If it is too tight it is difficult to obtain evenly spaced stitches. If it is too loose it will pucker. My goal when hand quilting is to have even stitches rather than small stitches.

If the quilt is to be machine quilted it will need to be pin basted. It is tempting to use the largest safety pins you can find, however, the bigger the pin the bigger the hole it leaves. I like to use the #1 size gilt safety pins. They are very sharp and make a nice small hole. Place the backing fabric, batting and quilt top as described above. Pin the quilt a hands-width apart, being careful not to place pins where the quilting lines are drawn.

Machine quilting requires that you roll the quilt to make it fit under the arm of the sewing machine. Rolling also makes it easier to turn. Anchor the quilt with a line quilted down the center in each direction, either straight or diagonally. Alternate the direction with every line. When doing free motion quilting, try using the slowest speed on the sewing machine and moving the quilt smoothly and evenly (like the Ouija Board pointer). There are several books available on machine quilting if you need help with this step.

THE QUILTS

The quilts in this book were all made using traditional quilt blocks. The fabrics are referred to as background and accent in the directions. The "one you love" may be either a background or an accent depending on the fabrics chosen. In the quilt diagrams the background will be shown in white and the foreground, or accent, will be colored.

I have taken classes from many wonderful quilters and read a zillion quilt books, so I cannot personally acknowledge every contribution to my education as a quilter. But I thank all of them for sharing with me so that I, in turn, can share with you and continue the tradition.

I hope that you will enjoy the Take 2 experience and look upon it as another patch on your quilt of life and not as the final word on the subject.

Irish Chain is an old favorite that is a perfect choice for Take 2. This one uses a 1" grid with 1-1/2" cut size for the strips. You can also vary the size of the squares to enlarge the quilt. Large florals are especially nice as backgrounds in this quilt.

IRISH CHAIN YARDAGE

LAP
45" X 65"
5 X 9 blocks

Accent	2-1/8 yds.
Background	1-3/4 yds.
Binding	1/2 yd.
Backing	2-7/8 yds.

DOUBLE
75" X 95"
11 x 15 blocks

Accent	4-5/8 yds.
Background	4-7/8 yds.
Binding	3/4 yd.
Backing	5-2/3 yds.

CUTTING

	Lap		Double	
Accent				
1-1/2" strips	24		67	
5-1/2" strips	6		9	
(outside border)				
Background				
1-1/2" strips	25		65	
3-1/2" strips	2		6	
5-1/2" strips	2		7	
into 3-1/2" x 5-1/2"		22		82
Binding - 2-1/2" strips	6		9	

CONSTRUCTION

1. Use the 1-1/2" strips to piece the two strip sets shown below. Make 3 (10 for a double) of Set 1 and 2 (7 for a double) of Set 2. Cross cut into 1-1/2" units. You will need 81 units (261) of Set 1 and 54 units (174) of Set 2.

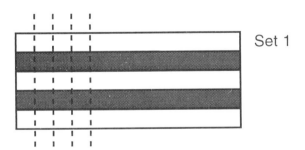

Set 1

Set 2

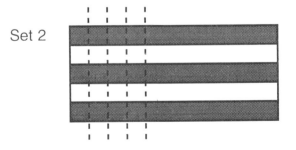

2. Construct 27 (87) "A" blocks with these units as shown below.

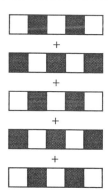

"A" Block

3. Using 1-1/2" strips of accent and 3-1/2" strips of background make 2 (6) of Set 3 as shown below. Cross cut into 44 (164) 1-1/2" units.

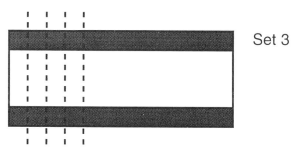

Set 3

4. Using these units and the 3-1/2" x 5-1/2" rectangles construct 22 (82) "B" blocks as shown.

5. Following the quilt diagram piece the blocks together, using the twosie-foursie method as explained on page 10.

6. The four "A" blocks left over will be used in the inside border. Using 1-1/2" strips make 4 (7) of Set 1. Measure the length and width of the top (measure the center not the edge). Cut the 2 widths and 2 lengths, piecing the strips when necessary. Attach the two length strips to the sides. Attach a block to each end of the two width strips then attach to the quilt top, matching seam lines at corners.

7. Attach the outside border.

Baste, quilt, bind and enjoy your quilt.

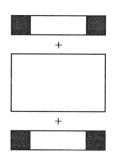

"B" Block

CHAPMAN COLLEGE
Northumberland Star

This quilt has a very antique look due to the fabrics chosen. It is almost entirely made up of Flying Geese. Janice's alma mater is "Chapman College" and these are the school colors, thus the name.

CUTTING

	Lap		Double	
Accent				
4-1/2" strips	10		31	
into 2-1/2" x 4-1/2"		144		436
into 4-1/2" square		2		18
remainder will be				
used in border				
Background				
14" strip			1	
into 14" squares				2
remainder into				
2-1/2" squares				25
25" strips	2		3	
* into 25" squares		2		3
into 2-1/2" strips then				
into 2-1/2" squares		120		180
2-1/2" strips	12		47	
into 2-1/2" squares		184		739
4-1/2" strips	4		14	
into 4-1/2" squares		22		76
into 2-1/2" x 4-1/2"		16		72
Binding - 2-1/2" strips	6		9	

*Because of the size of the triangles needed to square the quilt you must cut these first!

CONSTRUCTION

1. Make 144 (436 for the Double) Flying Geese Units (FGU) using the folded corner triangle method described on page 10.

2. For the Lap size make 2 blocks as shown at right. Then make 2 blocks as shown at the top of page 18, with an accent square in the center. For the Double make all 18 blocks with the accent fabric in the center, as shown at the top of page 18.

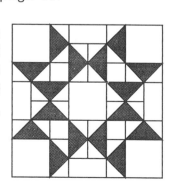

CHAPMAN COLLEGE YARDAGE

LAP
53" x 53"
4 blocks

Accent	1-3/8 yds.
Background	3 yds.
Binding	1/2 yd.
Backing	3-1/3 yds.

DOUBLE
75" x 98"
18 blocks

Accent	4-1/4 yds.
Background	8-1/4 yds.
Binding	3/4 yd.
Backing	5-7/8 yds.

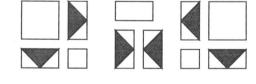

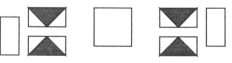

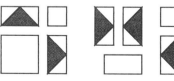

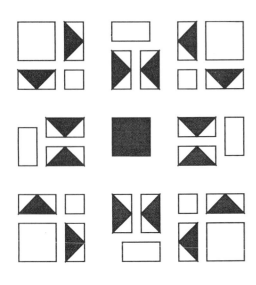

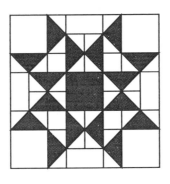

3. For the Lap Size sew the blocks together as shown in the quilt diagram on page 19. Cut the two 25" background squares in half diagonally and attach to the four block medallion to "square" it off.

4. For the Double cut the 14" background squares in half diagonally, these will be used for the corners. Cut the three 25" background squares in quarters diagonally to fill in the edges of the quilt. Lay out the quilt as shown in the diagram on page 16. Sew together in diagonal rows, placing the quarter-square triangles just cut at the ends of the rows as shown. Sew the rows together. Add the half-square triangles cut above to the four corners.

5. The Lap border is made by piecing 8 sets of 10 FGU each. Each side consists of two of these sets of FGU joined together with a rectangle of accent fabric to make the border strip the length needed. The size of the rectangle is determined as follows. Measure the inside dimensions of the quilt top as explained on page 11. Subtract the length of two FGU strips from this measurement. The difference, plus 1/2", is the length of the rectangle needed. Cut four rectangles from the 4-1/2" accent strip this length. Sew a rectangle between two FGU strips to make each border strip. Sew two borders on opposite sides. Attach two 4-1/2" background squares to the ends of the remaining border strips. Attach these strips to the other two sides.

6. The Double border is made using 4 sets of 16 FGU for the top and bottom borders, and 4 sets of 21 FGU for the side borders. Measure the quilt top as explained on page 11. For the top and bottom borders subtract the length of two 16 unit FGU strips from the width of the quilt. Cut two rectangles from the 4-1/2" accent strip this difference plus 1/2" for seam allowance. Sew a rectangle between two 16 unit FGU strips for both the top and the bottom. Attach to the quilt top and bottom. Repeat the above using the measurement for the length of the quilt, the 21 unit FGU strips and a rectangle of accent fabric. Add a 4-1/2" background to the ends of each of these two strips to complete the side borders. Sew to the sides of the quilt.

Baste, quilt, bind and you're finished!

19

STARK REALITY

Radiant Star is a pattern that I always wanted to make, but I thought it was beyond my skills as a piecer. However, it really is a piece of cake and one of the quickest quilts I have ever made.

CUTTING

Cut 15 strips from each color, 2-1/2" each.

For the binding cut six 2-1/2" strips.

STARK REALITY YARDAGE

WALLHANGING
59" x 59"

Accent	1-1/4 yds.
Background	3-1/8 yds.
Binding	1/2 yd.
Backing	3-5/8 yds.

CONSTRUCTION

1. Make five strip sets as follows. There are six strips, three of each color, in each of the strip sets. Begin with a background strip and sew an accent strip to it, off-setting it by 2". Make three pairs like this for each strip set. Next join the pairs, again off-setting by 2". In order to keep the strip set smooth and flat, sew every other seam in the opposite direction. Press all the seams in one direction.

2. Line up the sewn strip sets on a cutting mat (layer the strips if you are experienced with the rotary cutter). Place the 45° line of the ruler across the top edge. Cut the left edge at a 45° angle.

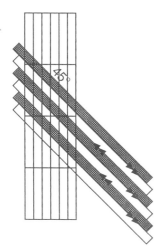

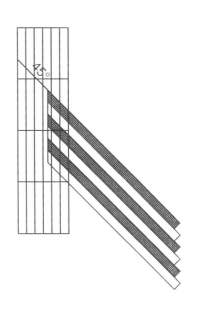

3. Move the ruler until the 2-1/2" line is at the 45° angle. Align the 45° mark on the ruler with the top straight edge. Cut, then measure off the next 2-1/2" mark. Continue cutting 2-1/2" units for a total of 48 units (star strips). You may need to recut the 45° angle periodically to keep the angle true.

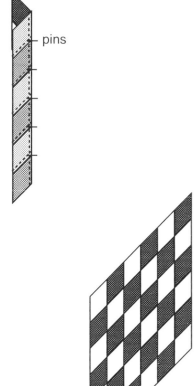

pins

4. Take two star strips. Turn one so the accent color is at the top and the other with the background color at the top. Place right sides together. Insert a pin through the seam allowance on the top strip at the first star point. Continue through the star point on the other strip. The pin should be through the cross of the seam allowance on both sides. Pin at all the star points. Sew one set together and check the matching of the points. If it is off, un-sew and practice until you can guesstimate the seam allowance. Handle the strips carefully, the edges are bias and can stretch and become distorted.

5. Sew strips together in sets of two, matching all points. Sew together three of these sets (six star strips in all) to make each diamond.

6. Check the 45° angle of the diamonds and trim lightly to size if too large. If smaller, re-press across the center and measure again. Trim if necessary. All diamonds should measure the same with a 1/4" variance.

7. Lay out the eight diamonds in a star shape. Mark each diamond at 1/4" from the tip and each corner.

8. Pin two diamonds together along inner seam, matching each star point. Start sewing 1/4" from outside edge and stop 1/4" from inside point.

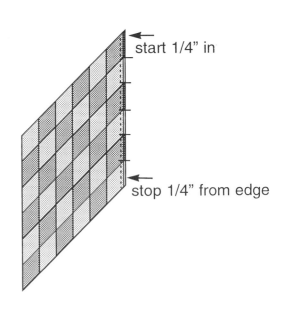

start 1/4" in

stop 1/4" from edge

9. Press on the wrong side. The two diamonds should now form a 90° angle. Use a 12" square ruler to square up the corner of the diamond points. Sew all four quarter units of the star together and check 90° angles.

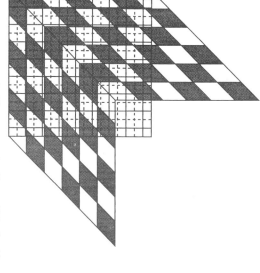

10. Sew the four sections together and then the two halves. Carefully pin the center seams and pin all star points. Sew from the center out and stop 1/4" from the outside edge.

11. Next find the bias (stretchy) and straight grain (non-stretchy) sides of the diamonds. Measure the length of all the straight grain sides from A to B, including the seam allowance, as shown below, to find the average diamond size. They should be within 1/4" of each other. The largest measurement is the size of the corner squares. It should be approximately 18". Cut four squares this size from the background fabric.

　　　To find the size of the edge triangles measure from B to B as shown below. Add 1-1/2" and cut one square this size from the background fabric. Cut diagonally from corner to corner in an "X".

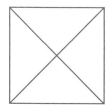

12. Sew the triangle units in first, starting with the bias sides of the diamonds first. Sew these with the diamond on the bottom. Pin in place and sew from the outside in and stop 1/4" from the inside point. Next sew the straight grain sides with the diamond on top and the triangle on the bottom. Try not to stretch any pieces as you ease in the bias sides. Sew in the corner squares in the same manner.

13. Square up the corners using a 1/2" seam allowance at the points of stars for a guide.

Baste, quilt, bind and enjoy your quilt!

HIDDEN STARS

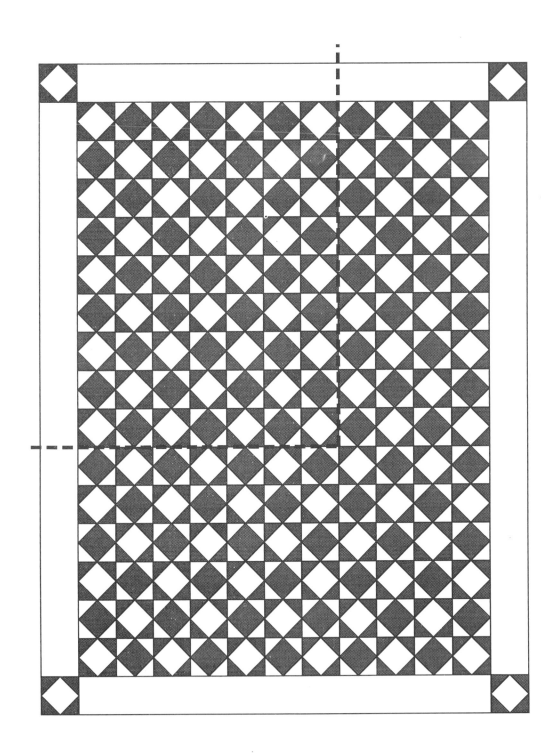

HIDDEN STARS

This quilt consists of only one block, but notice how the use of only two fabrics contributes to the design. Quick and easy, too!

CUTTING

	Wallhanging	Lap	Twin
Accent			
4-1/2" strips	2		
into 4-1/2" squares	18		
5-1/2" strips		5	12
into 5-1/2" squares		31	82
2-1/2" strips	5		
into 2-1/2" squares	72		
3" strips		11	25
into 3" squares		144	348
Background			
4-1/2" strips	2		
into 4-1/2" squares	18		
5-1/2" strips		6	13
into 5-1/2" squares		36	87
2-1/2" strips	5		
into 2-1/2" squares	72		
3" strips		9	24
into 3" squares		124	328
5-1/2" strips (border)		4	7
21" strip	1		
into 21" squares	2		
Binding - 2-1/2" strips	4	5	8

HIDDEN STARS YARDAGE

WALLHANGING
36" x 36"
6 x 6 blocks

Accent	3/4 yd.
Background	1-1/3 yds.
Binding	1/3 yd.
Backing	1-1/8 yds.

LAP
45" x 55"
7 x 9 blocks

Accent	1-7/8 yds.
Background	2-5/8 yds.
Binding	1/2 yd.
Backing	2-7/8 yds.

TWIN
65" x 85"
11 x 15 blocks

Accent	4-1/3 yds.
Background	5-5/8 yds.
Binding	5/8 yd.
Backing	5-1/8 yds.

CONSTRUCTION

"A" Block

"B" Block

Lap and Twin Size

1. Each block is built with four 3" squares and one 5-1/2" square. The smaller squares are cut from one fabric and the larger squares from the other. Attach the smaller squares to each corner of the large square using the Folded Corner Triangle Units method on page 10. Make 36 (87 for the twin) "A" blocks using large background squares and small accent squares. Also make 31 (82) "B" blocks using large accent squares and small background squares.

2. Arrange the blocks as shown in the diagram on page 24. Sew together using the twosie-foursie method on page 10.

3. There will be four blocks left over to be used as cornerstones for the border. Measure the length and width of the quilt (down and across the center). Piece the background border strips then cut two borders to the measured length. Attach to the sides of the quilt.

4. Cut two borders the measured width for the top and bottom. Attach the remaining blocks to each end of these and sew to the top and bottom.

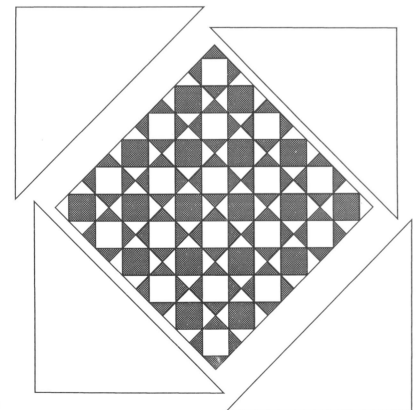

Wallhanging Size

5. Make 18 each of "A" and "B" blocks using the 2-1/2" and 4-1/2" squares.

6. Arrange as shown in the diagram at left and sew together using the twosie-foursie method.

7. Cut the 21" background squares in half diagonally. Sew one triangle to each corner. Square up the quilt top.

Baste, quilt, bind and enjoy your Hidden Stars!

Janice Minyard, Los Osos, Ca.

HIDDEN STARS

Pieced by Joanna Myrick,
Hand quilted by Joan Rexroth

MOCK CATHEDRAL
WINDOW

Joanna Myrick

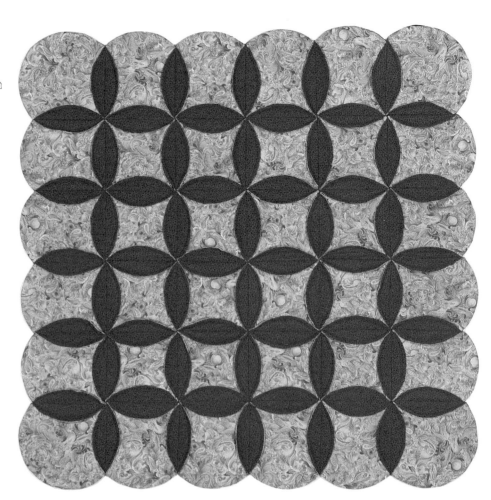

28

Pieced and Quilted by Stasi Roth. Joanna Myrick collection.

Linda Martin, Templeton, Ca.

Diana Imhoof, Atascadero, Ca.

Pieced and Quilted by Margaret Bailey, Stuart Bailey collection

Janice Minyard, Los Osos, Ca.

Pieced by Joanna Myrick, Quilted by Cheryl Cramer

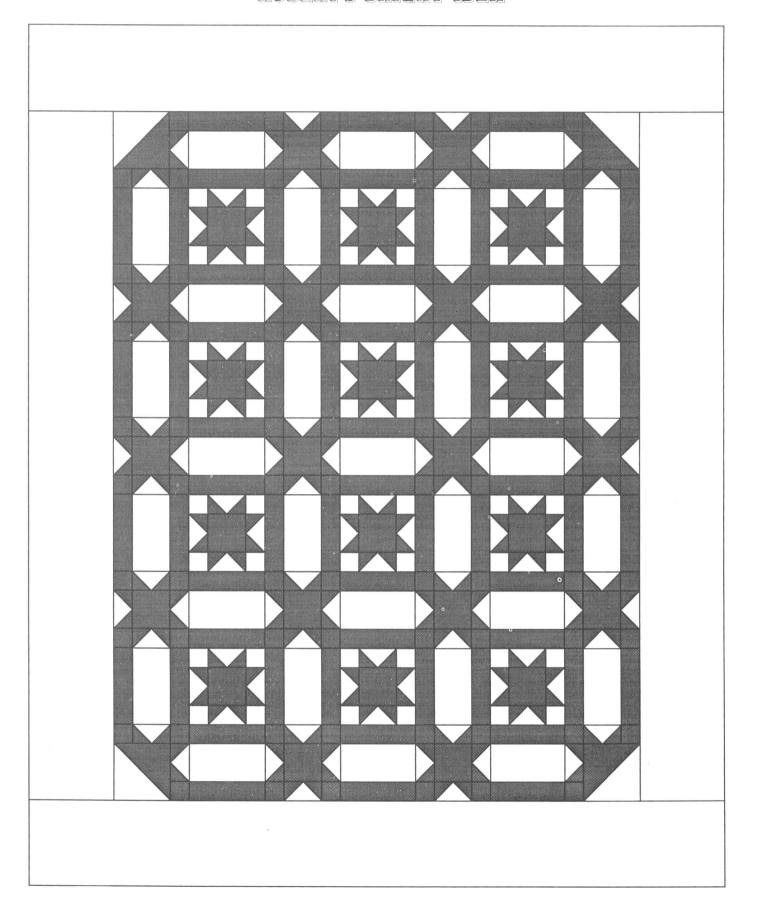

ROBERT'S BRIGHT IDEA YARDAGE

LAP

54" x 66"
7 x 9 blocks
(12 stars)

Accent	2-1/4 yds.
Background	2-7/8 yds.
Binding	1/2 yd.
Backing	3-3/8 yds.

DOUBLE/QUEEN

78" x 102"
11 x 15 blocks
(35 stars)

Accent	5-1/8 yds.
Background	5-5/8 yds.
Binding	3/4 yd.
Backing	6-1/8 yds.

ROBERT'S BRIGHT IDEA

This quilt is a very simple combination of two blocks. Linda's son, Robert, gave her the idea of the stars, thus the name. We've nicknamed it RBI.

CUTTING

	Lap		Double/Queen	
Accent				
2" strips	16		40	
into 2" squares		316		836
3-1/2" strips	3		7	
into 3-1/2" squares		28		79
2" strips	12		28	
5-3/8" strips	1		1	
into 5-3/8" squares		2		2
Background				
2" strips	3		7	
into 2" squares		48		140
3-1/2" strips	6		16	
into 2" x 3-1/2"		120		324
3-1/2" strips	6		14	
6-1/2" strips (border)	6		9	
5-3/8" strip	1		1	
into 5-3/8" squares		2		2
Binding - 2-1/2" strips	6		9	

CONSTRUCTION

1. Make 120 (324 for the Double/Queen) Flying Geese Units (FGU) with the 2" x 3-1/2" background rectangles and the 2" accent squares. Use the folded corner triangle unit instructions on page 10.

2. Make 16 (44) of "A" block using the FGU made above, the 3-1/2" accent squares, and the 2" accent squares.

"A" Block

3. Make 12 (35) of "B" block using the FGU made above, the 3-1/2" accent squares, and the 2" background squares.

"B" Block

4. Make 6 (14) strip sets as shown below using 3-1/2" background strips and 2" accent strips. Cross cut strip sets into 6-1/2" blocks. This is Block C (rail block); make 31 (82) of them.

"C" Block

5. Layer each 5-3/8" background square right sides together with a 5-3/8" accent square. Draw a diagonal across the lighter square. Sew 1/4" along each side of the diagonal line. Cut on the line and press open.

6. Make four Corner Blocks using the half-square triangles just made, FGU, and 2" squares of accent fabric as shown below.

7. Lay out the blocks as shown in the diagram then sew together.

Corner Block

8. Attach the 6-1/2" borders following the directions on page 11.

Baste, quilt, bind and enjoy!

PINEAPPLE QUILT

PINEAPPLE QUILT

Pineapple quilts are a variation of the Log Cabin block and pieced much the same way by adding "logs." Pineapples are pieced in the Courthouse Steps method of Log Cabin and though they look difficult they are really simple and quite impressive.

CUTTING

	Lap		King	
Accent				
2-1/4" strips	3		14	
into 2-1/4" squares		50		242
2-7/8" strips	4		18	
into 2-7/8" squares		50		242
3-3/8" strips	5		21	
into 3-3/8" squares		50		242
1" strips (2nd border)	5		10	
* 1-1/2" strips	16		76	
Background				
2-1/2" strips	2		8	
into 2-1/2" squares		25		121
1-1/2" strips	44		195	
(includes 1st border)				
* 3/4" strips	8		38	
4-1/2" strips (3rd border)	6		11	
Binding - 2-1/2" strips	6		11	

*See note in step 9 before cutting.

CONSTRUCTION

1. Draw an "X" across both diagonals and a cross from side to side on the wrong side of each 2-1/2" background square. The intersection is the "squaring point" for all the blocks. After each row and each set of corners are added the corners will be cut off (nubbed) using the squaring point as a point of reference. This is explained in detail in step 4 below.

2. Cut 2-1/4" accent squares in half diagonally. Attach two triangles to opposite corners of each 2-1/2" background square. Press open, then attach triangles to the other two sides. Press.

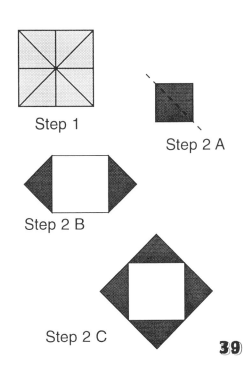

Step 1

Step 2 A

Step 2 B

Step 2 C

39

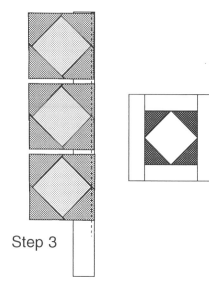

Step 3

3. Sew all blocks, face down, to a 1-1/2" background strip leaving about 1/8" between blocks. Trim and press. Repeat for opposite side. Repeat again for third and fourth sides. Trim and press open.

4. Place ruler with the 2-1/4" mark at the "squaring point", lining up the lines on the ruler with the drawn lines on the background square. Cut off the corners on two sides as shown below. Turn and repeat on the other two corners. The block will now be eight-sided and about 4-1/2".

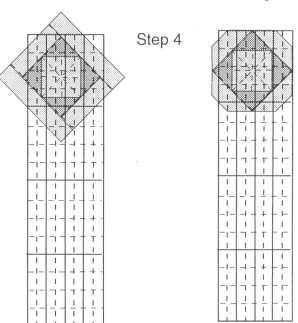

Step 4

Step 5 A

Step 5 B

5. Cut 2-7/8" accent squares in half diagonally. Center on long sides of block, sew on, then press open. The squaring point is 3-1/4". Line up the ruler with the 3-1/4" mark on the squaring point and nub the corners. Turn the block around and repeat. The block is about 5-1/4".

Step 5 C

6. Sew all blocks, face down, to 1-1/2" background strips as in Step # 3. Trim and press open. The squaring point is 3-1/4". Line up the ruler and nub the corners. Turn and repeat. The block now measures about 6-1/2".

7. Cut 3-3/8" accent squares in half diagonally. Center on the long sides of the blocks, stitch, and press open. Use a squaring point of 4-1/4" to nub the corners. Turn and repeat. The block will measure approximately 7-1/4".

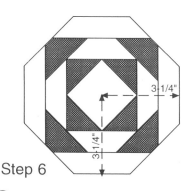

Step 6

8. Sew all blocks to 1-1/2" background strips as in Step # 3. Trim and press open. Nub the corners using a 4-1/4" squaring point. Turn and repeat. The block is about 8-1/2".

9. To get the narrow strip of background in the corner the final corner triangles must be pieced. Make 8 (38 for the King) strip sets using a 1-1/2" strip of accent, a 3/4" strip of background, and another 1-1/2" strip of accent as shown here.

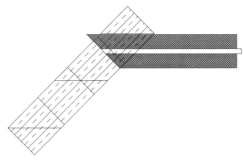

Step 7

Use the 45° degree line on the rotary ruler to cut triangles out of the strip sets. The Lap size uses 100 triangles; the King, 484. Each strip set will yield 13 triangles.

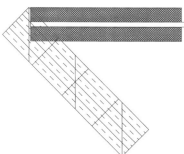 

Sew these triangles to the corners of the block. The outside (short) edges of the triangles are bias, handle them carefully so they don't stretch. Do not nub the corners, the block is complete. It should be about 9-1/4" square.

Step 8

Note: If you prefer to have plain corner blocks, cut 5 (25 for the King) 3-7/8" strips of accent fabric instead of the 1-1/2" accent strips and the 3/4" background strips. Cross cut these into 50 (242) squares, 3-7/8" each. Cut these squares diagonally and proceed as described above.

Step 9

10. Arrange blocks in five rows of five. Sew together using the twosie-foursie method explained on page 10. Measure the middle both ways and cut the first border to size. Sew sides on first, then the top and bottom. Measure again and cut second border. Again sew sides first then the top and bottom. Repeat for the third border.

Baste, quilt, bind and enjoy your Pineapple quilt!

41

HOUSEWIFE'S REVENGE

This was one of the first Take 2 quilts designed with this book in mind. We can't remember where the name came from but the block is a variation of Jacob's Ladder. We celebrate First Friday at our shop with open sewing in the classroom. It gets a little silly sometimes so perhaps that is where the name came from. Again the simplicity of the design complements the two fabric scheme.

CUTTING

		Lap		Double	
Accent					
	3-7/8" strips	5		14	
	into 3-7/8" squares		48		140
	2" strips	5		14	
	into 2" squares		96		280
	3-7/8" strips (pieced border)**	4		6	
	**into 3-7/8" squares		32		52
Background					
	3-1/2" strips	8		24	
	into 3-1/2" squares		96		280
	2-3/8" strips	6		17	
	into 2-3/8" squares		96		280
	3-1/2" strips (border)	5		8	
	into 3-1/2" squares*		4		4
	3-7/8" strips (pieced border)**	4		6	
	**into 3-7/8" squares		32		52
Binding - 2-1/2" strips		6		9	

*These strips are used for the inner border as well as for the corners of the outer border.

**These are for half-square triangles. Before cutting decide how you wish to make these units. If using a grid or triangle paper don't cut the strips or squares, as you'll need the larger piece of fabric to do them. See page 9.

HOUSEWIFE'S REVENGE YARDAGE

LAP
48" x 60"
3 x 4 blocks

Accent	1-1/2 yds.
Background	2-3/8 yds.
Binding	1/2 yd.
Backing	3 yds.

DOUBLE
72" x 96"
5 x 7 blocks

Accent	3-3/8 yds.
Background	5-1/2 yds.
Binding	3/4 yd.
Backing	5-3/4 yds.

CONSTRUCTION

1. Cut the 2-3/8" background squares and 48 (140 for the double) of the 3-7/8" accent squares in half diagonally.

2. Stitch two of these background triangles to the sides of a 2" accent square as shown. Make 96 (280) of these units.

3. Attach the accent triangle as illustrated here.

4. Piece together 12 (35) of the blocks at left using eight of these pieced units and eight 3-1/2" background squares for each block.

5. Arrange the blocks according to the diagram then sew together using the twosie-foursie method explained on page 10.

6. Attach the inside border using 3-1/2" background strips and following the directions for borders on page 11.

7. For the outside border make half square triangles using the method you prefer from page 9. The finished size is 3", so either use a grid or cut squares that measure 3-7/8". The lap size requires 64 half square triangles, the double uses 104. Sew these together in pairs to form a rectangle as shown below. You will need 7 rectangle units each for the top and bottom and 9 for each side (11 and 15 for the double). Sew them together in rows.

8. Sew on the side borders. Next sew the 3-1/2" background squares to the top and bottom rows of rectangle units. Finally sew the top and bottom borders on, matching the seam points at the cornerstones.

Baste, quilt, bind and enjoy!

RAD TRIANGLES

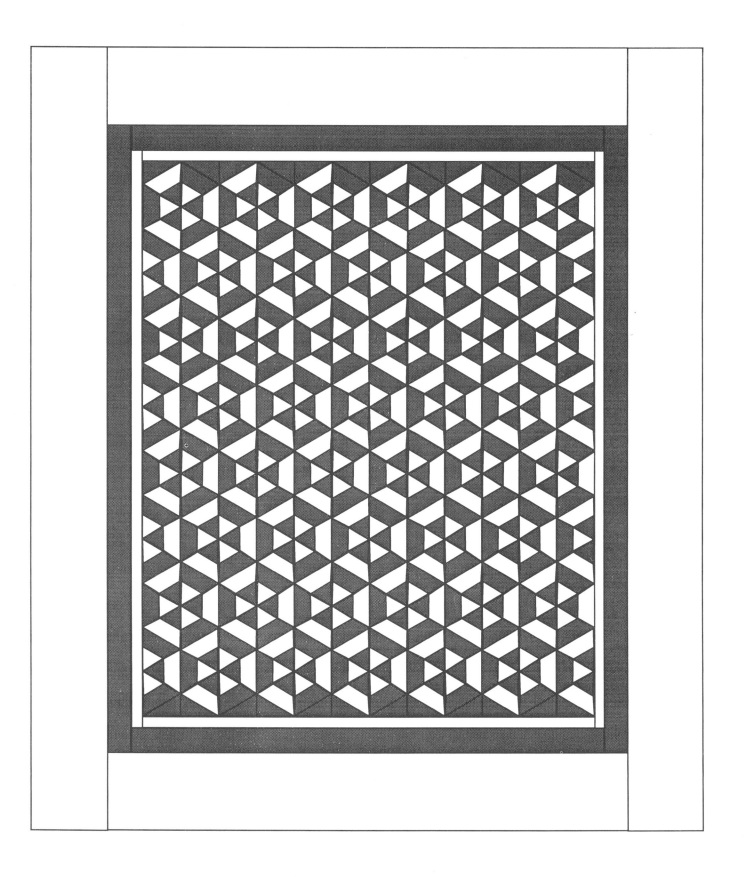

RAD TRIANGLES YARDAGE

LAP
58" x 67"
288 blocks

Accent	1-3/4 yds.
Background	2-5/8 yds.
Binding	5/8 yd.
Backing	3-5/8 yds.

TWIN
58" x 93"
432 blocks

Accent	2-1/2 yds.
Background	3-5/8 yds.
Binding	5/8 yd.
Backing	5-1/3 yds.

RAD TRIANGLES

Margaret and her husband, Stuart, work in the nuclear power industry. She made this quilt for Stuart because it reminded her of the radiation symbol which is a major part of their lives.

CUTTING

	Lap	Twin
Accent		
2-1/4" strips	18	27
4-3/8" strip	1	1
2-1/4" strips (second border)	5	7
Background		
2-1/4" strips	18	27
1-1/4" strips (first border)	5	6
6" strips (third border)	6	8
Binding - 2-1/2" strips	7	8

CONSTRUCTION

1. Use the 2-1/4" strips to construct 18 (27 for the Twin) sets of strips as shown below. Press seam toward the darkest strip.

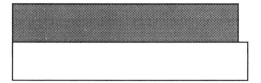

2. Cut the strips into 288 (432) equilateral triangles using a 60° triangle "ruler" as shown below. Or use the 60° line on the rotary ruler. Each strip should yield 16 triangles.

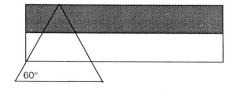
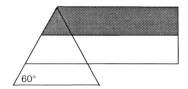
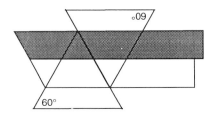

3. The quilt top is constructed in vertical rows. The end of each row is 1/2 of an equilateral triangle. Cut twelve 60° triangles from the 4-3/8" accent strip. Cut each one in half as illustrated.

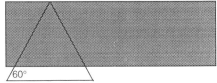

4. Lay out the triangles as shown below. There are 24 (36) pieced triangles in each row. Make six of Row A and six of Row B. Begin and end each row with the accent triangle cut in Step 3 above. Sew triangles together.

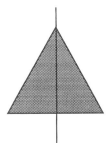

Row A

Row B

Continue the pattern.

5. Sew the rows together.

6. Measure the center of the quilt in both directions, width and length.

7. Attach the first border using 1-1/4" background strips and the directions on page 11.

8. Sew on the second border using the 2-1/4" accent strips.

9. Add the third border using the 6" background strips.

Baste, quilt, bind and enjoy.

STARRY NIGHTS & IRISES

The Log Cabin Block is one of my favorite because of its versatility. It is a wonderful vehicle for Take 2 and offers a great many sets to choose from. Our set is barn-raising.

CUTTING

	Lap	Double
Accent		
1-1/4" strips	31	121
Background		
1-1/4" strips	24	93
6-1/2" strips (border)	5	8
Binding		
2-1/2" strips	5	9

CONSTRUCTION

1. Sew a 1-1/4" background and a 1-1/4" accent strip together. Make two sets for the lap quilt and six sets for the double. Cross cut into 1-1/4" units. Cut 48 units for the lap size and 192 for the double. The remainder of the block is built by sewing your "logs" to the "cabin" and trimming.

2. Place the units just made on a background strip, right sides together, with the accent fabric square towards you. Place them one behind the other, chaining all these units through, allowing a small space (1/8") between each new unit. Press and cut apart.

STARRY NIGHTS & IRISES YARDAGE

LAP
44" x 54"
6 x 8 blocks

Accent	1-1/4 yds.
Background	2 yds.
Binding	1/2 yd.
Backing	2-3/4 yds.

DOUBLE
75" X 96"
12 X 16 blocks

Accent	4-5/8 yds.
Background	5-1/4 yds.
Binding	3/4 yd.
Backing	5-3/4 yds.

3. The next two strips will be the accent fabric. Attach the cabin units with the last piece sewn placed away from you. Press and cut apart. The fourth and fifth strips will be the background fabric. Continue in this manner, adding two strips of each color and alternating as shown in the diagram. Remember to always keep the last log sewn face down and away from you and your rotation will not get mixed up. There are six background logs and seven accent logs, counting the center. The last strip sewn will be the accent fabric. Press after every log and trim to square block.

   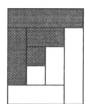

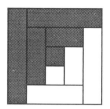 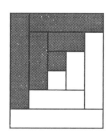 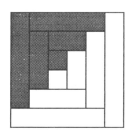 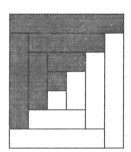

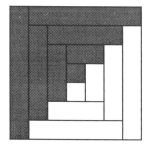

4. Arrange the blocks as shown in the diagram (barn-raising). Sew together using the twosie-foursie method explained on page 10. The lap quilt has 48 blocks and the double quilt has 192 blocks.

5. Attach 6-1/2" border strips to the sides according to the directions on page 11. Press and attach the top and bottom border strips.

Baste, quilt, bind and enjoy your Log Cabin quilt!

GEORGIA ON MY MIND YARDAGE

WALLHANGING
44" x 70"

Accent	* 1-1/2 yds.
Background	3 yds.
Binding	1/2 yd.
Backing	2-3/4 yds.

* This allows 1/2 yd. for the medallion. You may need more or less depending on the design and fabric chosen.

"Georgia On My Mind" is very special to me. It is the first quilt that I "designed" and the inspiration for this book. It represents a lot of personal growth and gave my self-esteem a large boost by placing first in the small quilt division at the 1993 American International Quilt Festival, in Houston.

CUTTING

	Wallhanging	
Background and Accent		
2-7/8" strips	4	
into 2-7/8" squares		48
3-3/8" strips	2	
into 3-3/8" squares		14
5-1/4" strip	1	
into 5-1/4" squares		6
Accent only		
4-1/2" strip	1	
into 4-1/2" squares		3
Background only		
4-1/2" strips	2	
into 4-1/2" squares		12
2-1/2" strips	2	
** 3" strip	1	
5-1/2" strips	4	
into 5-1/2" squares		2
** into 4" x 12-1/2"		2
10" strip	1	
into 10" square		2
into 8" square		2
22-1/2" strip	1	
*** into 22-1/2" square		1
into 16" square		1
Binding		
2-1/2" strips	6	

** These are used to adjust the width of a row and may vary slightly from this size. Cut them as you need them and check the necessary size first.

*** This is used for the medallion if you applique onto the background. See Step 1 under Quilt Top on page 53.

CONSTRUCTION

Blocks

1. To make the small pinwheels use the 2-7/8" accent and background squares to make half-square triangles as explained on page 9. Make 24 small pinwheels as shown at right using four of these half-square triangle units for each.

Steps 1 & 2

2. Make seven large pinwheels following the directions above and using the 3-3/8" squares of both fabrics.

3. Make three Ohio Star blocks as follows. Sew quarter-square triangle units using the 5-1/4" accent and background squares and the instructions on page 9. Lay out the blocks according to the diagram at right. Each block uses four half-square triangle units, one 4-1/2" square of accent fabric and four 4-1/2" squares of background fabric. Sew in rows and press the seam allowances toward the unpieced squares. Finally sew the rows together.

Step 3

Quilt Top

1. Select a medallion for the center of your quilt. It could be an appliqued motif from the primary fabric (as I used) or a pieced square. The medallion should be 22-1/2" (22" finished) square.

2. Sew the small pinwheels together into two rows of five and two rows of seven. Sew the two shorter rows together lengthwise. Attach to the bottom, left edge of the medallion. Sew the longer rows together and attach to the bottom, right edge of the medallion.

3. Sew 2-1/2" strips of background fabric to the top edges of the medallion. Press under the seam allowance on two adjacent sides of a large pinwheel. Line up the pinwheel in the top corner of the medallion and applique in place along the pressed edges.

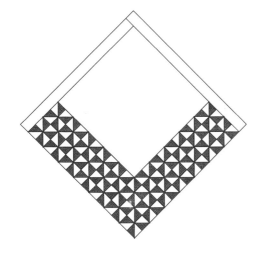

4. Cut a 5-1/2" background strip in half. Sew a large pinwheel between the two halves.   Make two of these.

5. Sew one of these strips onto the top left edge of the medallion, placing the pinwheel approximately 8" from the top corner. Trim the strip at the top corner. Repeat with the other strip on the top right edge.

6. Trim the lower ends of the strip by placing the 45° line of the ruler against the small pinwheels and trimming along the straight edge about 1" from the edge of the pinwheels.

7. Cut the 16" background square in half diagonally. Center and sew one half to the upper left edge of the medallion. Sew the other half to the upper right edge. Trim the right and left sides even with the previously trimmed strips. Trim the top to approximately 1" above the centered pinwheel. Make sure the top is at a right angle to the sides.

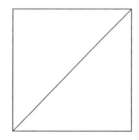

8. Sew two large pinwheels and two 5-1/2" background squares together into a 4-patch.

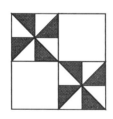

9. Cut two 8" squares of background in half diagonally and sew to the 4-patch as shown here.

10. Now sew the following together in a row. Ohio Star block, a 3" (or the width needed to make this section the same width as the medallion section) strip of background, the 4-patch pinwheel block, another 3" strip of background and another Ohio Star block. Center the 4-patch block vertically between the Ohio Stars.

11. Trim the top and bottom of the 4-patch unit even with the top and bottom of the Ohio Star blocks.

12. Center and sew this section to the top of the medallion section.

13. Cut a 5-1/2" background strip into quarters (5-1/2" x 10-1/2"). Sew each of these to opposite sides of two pinwheel blocks.

14. Cut two 10" background squares in half diagonally. Center and sew each of these to the other sides of the two pinwheel blocks. Trim to make 12-1/2" blocks.

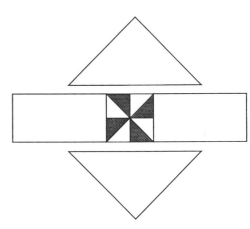

15. Sew the pinwheel blocks made above to opposite sides of an Ohio Star block. Cut and sew 4" (or the width necessary to make this section the same width as the bottom section) background strips to the sides of this unit.

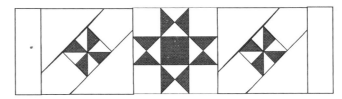

16. Center and sew this section on top of the previously sewn sections.

The quilt top is now complete. Baste, quilt, bind and you're finished!

MOCK CATHEDRAL WINDOW

MOCK CATHEDRAL WINDOW

This quilt has been a favorite at Quiltworks because when you get it done, it's done! It's pieced, quilted, backed and bound all at the same time. The size is easy to adapt by changing the size of the circles. It's a great beginner quilt and very impressive at all levels!

CUTTING

Cut both fabrics and filling into 10" squares. You will need 48 (117) squares of each.

CONSTRUCTION

1. Cut a circle from template plastic using the template on page 59. Trace around the circle on the wrong side of the accent fabric. This will be the sewing line. Use a marking tool that you can see clearly on your fabric since it will not show.

2. Layer the squares in the following order, right sides together: filling, background fabric, and accent fabric. Sew completely around the circle on the drawn line, using a slightly smaller than normal stitch.

3. Press each unit and trim around the sewn line using pinking shears. The pinking shears eliminate clipping of curves.

4. Make a small slit approximately 1" from the top of the background fabric. Reach inside and pull the right sides through.

5. Finger press the seam from the inside using a smooth instrument. Press. My friends call these my potholders. It is a very boring quilt to construct at this point. But hang in there for the fun! Since we are dealing with layers of fabric the next step is not an exact measure.

MOCK CATHEDRAL WINDOW YARDAGE		
LAP		
42" x 55"		
6 x 8 blocks		
Accent		3-3/4 yds.
Background		3-3/4 yds.
Filling*		3-3/4 yds.
TWIN		
62" X 88"		
9 X 13 blocks		
Accent		9-1/4 yds.
Background		9-1/4 yds.
Filing*		9-1/4 yds.

*Must be able to withstand pressing - we used Thermore. Flannel will also work, but is very heavy.

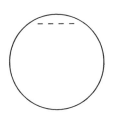

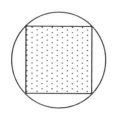

6. Begin with a 6-1/2" square cut from the template plastic. Place it in the center of the background side of the "potholder" as shown and mark around all four sides. This will be the next sewing line. It is important that the marked point of the square match the outside of the circle. You may need to trim the square slightly to allow for the thickness of the marking pencil. Try to trim evenly to keep the template square.

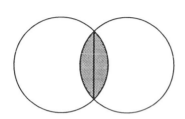

7. Sew the units (potholders) together in pairs. With accent sides together match the sewing lines and in the center as well. Sew across. You will need to anchor the stitching at the start and finish by back stitching. It is very important that the two pieces line up exactly. You will probably need to release your pins at the start and finish to allow this to happen. Ease in any excess fabric. Finger press the flaps down. (I always sew the sides with the slits together first. That way I know the slits will be covered when the flaps are sewn down, and I don't have to worry about them.)

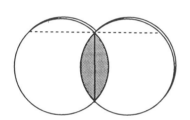

8. Next sew pairs of pairs together. Carefully match and pin the start and finish and the seam in the middle. Sew this seam, again anchoring the beginning and ending. When sewing across the seam be careful not to catch the flap. You really want to aim for the edge and have one stitch actually fall between the two pieces. I found that sometimes I need to not follow my marked sewing line in order to match the seam. If you are too far away you will have a hole. If you sew across the flaps it will not lie flat.

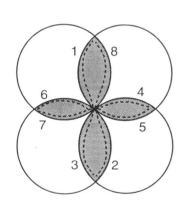

9. Press the "foursies". You will "quilt" these now by topstitching the flaps down, which will hide the slits. Begin with a stitch length of 0 and slowly increase the length to your normal length. End the stitching the same way by decreasing back to 0. (This should take about 1/2"). Follow the quilting directions at left and you can do all the flaps with only one start and finish.

10. Sew all units using the twosie-foursie method and quilt. When all the units are together top stitch the outside edge to finish.

No need to baste, quilt or bind, it's done. Enjoy!

Template for
Mock Cathedral Window

place on fold

AMEN CORNER
THE LAST WORD...

It seems that many of us obsess over making the "perfect" quilt and lose all sense of joy in the creation of them. We must allow ourselves to appreciate the process of learning the craft. As we progress along the journey we need to accept our work as being the best that we can do, at this time. Quilting, like playing a musical instrument, takes practice, practice, practice. It is wonderful to watch our piecing improve and our stitches grow smaller and more even with every project we complete.

Let's pat ourselves on the back and appreciate the hard work that we have invested in each and every project. Let's challenge ourselves to do different kinds of piecing and quilting. Let's just do it for ourselves and remember, it doesn't matter if any one else like our quilts, it only matters that we like them!

Now, hold your head up high, thrust your fist in the air, say "Yes!" and do the dance of happiness. You did it!

Other books by **ANIMAS QUILTS PUBLISHING**

WEAVER FEVER by Jackie Robinson $ 6.50
    Bargello type quilts in a woven design. Easy.

QUADCENTRICS by Jackie Robinson $ 7.00
    Designs which travel over and under each other.

TESSELLATIONS by Jackie Robinson $ 12.00
    Geometric shapes forming a repeating pattern.
    Inspired by M.C. Escher.

ON THE DOUBLE by Suzan Drury $ 14.00
    Two-for-one quilts cut from one basic strip set.

DINING DAZZLE by Jackie Robinson $ 16.00
    A collection of 20 placemats and 4 table runners.

REFLECTIONS by Melinda Malone $ 13.00
    Positive-negative designs in great quilts.

SIMPLY LANDSCAPES by Judy Sisneros $ 14.00
    Turn your favorite scene into a quilt with ease.

APPLIQUE, THE EASY WAY
    by Kathryn Kuhn and Timmie Stewart
    No basting or pressing with this easy method. $ 20.00

PERENNIAL PATCHWORK by Jackie Robinson $ 11.00
    A garden of flower blocks in eight different "sets".

STAR GAZING by Jackie Robinson $ 12.00
    Ohio stars in several variations.

CHAINS OF LOVE by Jackie Robinson $ 10.00
    Double and Triple Irish Chain quilts.

BINDING MITER TOOL $ 4.00
    Make mitered corners on quilt bindings
    easy and perfect every time.

PLEASE ADD POSTAGE:

$ 1.25 FOR 1 ITEM
$ 2.25 FOR 2 - 4 ITEMS
$ 3.25 FOR 5 - 9 ITEMS

THANK YOU!

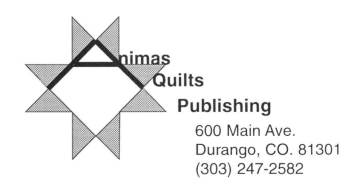

Animas
Quilts
Publishing
600 Main Ave.
Durango, CO. 81301
(303) 247-2582